A Month of Sundays

Colorful Stories of God's Providence & Humor

Harold L. Bare, Sr. Ph.D.
Laila B. Bare, Ed. D.

A Month of Sundays
By Harold L. Bare, Sr. Ph.D.
© 2008 All rights reserved.

No part of this publication may be reproduced or transmitted in any form or by any means, mechanical or electronic, including photocopying and recording, or by any information storage and retrieval system, without permission in writing from author or publisher (except by a reviewer, who may quote brief passages and/or show brief video clips in a review).

ISBN: 978-0-9817009-1-5 (13 digit)
ISBN: 0-9817009-1-8 (10 digit)

Published by:

www.AuthorsPublisher.com
info@AuthorsPublisher.com

Cover & Interior Designs by:

Megan Johnson
Johnson2Design
www.Johnson2Design.com
megan@Johnson2Design.com

Dedication

Forty-four years ago I looked across a college cafeteria to see a young woman. "I will get to know her better," I whispered to myself. Three years later we were married. Every challenge of life since that time we have shared.

Laila has never allowed me to take the easy road. On our first date she dared to embarrass me in presence of fraternity brothers by bowling a higher score. To this day she will win any game if possible and just say: "If you are a man you can take it."

Once I offered to her that it might be best for me to give up on earning a doctorate at the University of Virginia. Course work was done, but the dissertation process was lingering. Laila listened and responded: "Just answer me one question. You said that God told you to earn a doctorate. When did God change his mind?"

I am still fascinated with Laila. Grateful to her. Yes, I acknowledge that the finished product of this book probably has more hours of her time than mine. Rightly so I dedicate this book to Dr. Laila B. Bare, the love of my life.

Acknowledgements

To acknowledge is not to pay a debt, for some debts cannot be repaid. Words of appreciation are not equal to kindness and love freely given.

Laila and I recognize the treasure of having been children in pastors' homes. From our birth we both were blessed with godly parents who gave sacrificially in ministry. The integrity of their lives vested us with a simple faith to trust God during our pastoral experiences.

We ever hold in esteem and gratitude our children who have lived with parents driven to pursue ministry. Harold, II (Danny), Dana, and Joshua have lived their lives in the context of ministry. All three deeply love the Lord.

We are eternally indebted to the kind people of Wytheville Church of God [now Maranatha], Wytheville, VA, and Covenant Church of God, Charlottesville, VA, for their allowing us to serve them.

Our debt to Our Lord for the privilege of serving in ministry is too great to express in words. We have found life's greatest treasures in serving others.

Introduction

Being a pastor is one of the noblest, yet humblest tasks given by God to man. It has the highest and lowest moments of life all wrapped up in one package. Without laughter the burden and stress wear upon a minister until the hues of a rainbow are blended into pastel colors.

Two motivations have driven Laila and me in the writing of these short stories. First, we believe these stories happen to ministers and lay people. Our hope is that as you read these stories you will often insert yourself as the lead character.

We have found that our humanity tends to keep us from seeing the humor that we think causes God and angels to chuckle. Long after events happen we look back and laugh at what was grievous or frightening at the time of the story. Candidly, our ego tends to contaminate at the time of events.

A second motivation is to suggest to seasoned ministers the virtue of growing older full of wonder for the journey. Younger ministers are not attracted to ministry by older ministers who with the years allow the wick of the candle to burn low and feeble. Younger ministers are drawn to and want to be mentored by older ministers who have delighted themselves in the Lord, loved being in ministry---challenges included.

Finally, ministry has no beginning and ending. Once Laila and I drove many miles from our parish into a remote part of the hills. An old store along a river still had ladders on wheels that rolled on tracks along walls stacked with merchandise from floor to ceiling.

We were in a strange little town. I decided to look for a pair of shoes. As the store manager worked the shoe on my foot he said: "Reverend, how is your church doing?" Turns out his sister sent him the weekly paper from our town. He knew all about Laila and me.

In ministry there is no time off. Every day is Sunday.

Table of Contents

1.	My Blue Goose	1
2.	That Ole Swing	5
3.	Hank Snow	9
4.	The Auction	13
5.	God Told Me	17
6.	Having Church	21
7.	Intellectual Capacity	25
8.	Competition	29
9.	Change	31
10.	Tom	35
11.	Never On A Sunday	39
12.	The Lawyer	43
13.	Methodist Neighbor	47
14.	Oh, So Smart	51
15.	Jerry	55
16.	A Visit to a Factory	59
17.	The Red Carpet	63

18.	Nightmare	67
19.	The Baptism	71
20.	Six Dollars and Thirty-Seven Cents	75
21.	Surprise Miracles	79
22.	The Red Necktie	83
23.	Wendall	87
24.	Talking to the Bishop	91
25.	The Newcomer	95
26.	That Woman	99
27.	World's Worst Sermon	103
28.	We Never Cancel	107
29.	Big Red	111
30.	Running Away	115

Day 1
My Blue Goose

Our attendance had grown from 17 to 50. I needed a booster shot. Laila and I agreed to make a huge personal sacrifice of about $250 for me to attend a church growth conference in Atlanta, about 300 miles away.

A pastor of a small congregation understands that growth needs finances. If the pastor gets all the money, the church cannot grow.

I carpooled to Atlanta and shared a motel room, thus saving on cost. That left me the cost of registration and eating.

Sitting in a large auditorium I was a blank page to be written on by powerful speakers who apparently had been God's chosen wise pastors. They had no stories to tell of failures. Oh, what giants they were. I had come because of my failures and deep consciousness of a lack of knowing how to do what was in my heart as a pastor.

The bus preacher came along. He told marvelous stories that convinced me there could be no future for a local church without a bus ministry. There was a lot of laughter when he shared about a Sunday morning when church buses from Lynchburg, Virginia met church buses from Houston, Texas on the same street in Akron, Ohio as they were picking up passengers. His message was clear: The future of church growth belonged to pastors and churches that developed bus ministry! One could easily infer from his enthusiasm that buses might be picking up saints in the Rapture.

Not much given to follow fads or fashions, I listened and thought it over. Maybe there was logic to the message. About halfway back to Virginia we stopped in Gastonia, North Carolina. Beside the road was a 60 passenger bus for sale for only $300. It had to be divine!

It was an excellent bus, painted blue and white. Good motor. Good tires. How I paid for it I do not remember. My friends went on in the car. I drove the Blue Goose home with every mile bringing me closer to the blessings of a bus ministry, a growing church, and acceptance into the club of the wise and courageous pastors who were determined to give every person in America a free ride to church.

Laila was excited with me. We have always been a team to cast vision and seek out viable methods of ministry.

The first problem that arose was that we had no place to park the bus. Most of the time it sat on the street in front of our home, looking bigger than our church building. The church parking lot was too small for the bus.

The second problem was that we had no driver and worker to find and pick up people on the bus. The third problem was that we had no mechanic for repairs. The fourth problem was that we had not figured on the cost of insurance. We had also not counted on the cost of gasoline, though cheaper in those days, when every dollar was precious.

Day One

We named the bus "The Blue Goose." It served its best purpose when snow came. It was the only vehicle in the neighborhood that could go to town. I did enjoy those drives. Little did I know that one day the Blue Goose would ride me right into trouble.

Gradually it dawned on us that no one was going to be interested in doing the bus ministry. That was not a terrible disappointment. If we had filled the bus up our little building would not have been big enough to hold the people.

In truth the Blue Goose became an embarrassment. The letters on the side inviting people to church had no realistic meaning. A vehicle with engine and good tires just sat on the side of the road. One of the best days of my life was the day we sold the Blue Goose.

Many Sundays have passed since the Blue Goose was sold. Fads and techniques have come and gone with the Sundays. At any given moment in time there seems to be a conference with some hero who has never had a failure. Those who are willing to pay a registration fee and buy books and materials can buy into the current "Blue Goose."

Whatever happened to preaching the Word, loving people, and asking God for wisdom? Why do pastors too often feel compelled to emulate what God has given to another pastor in another city for another people?

I fear too many pastors buy a Blue Goose. I am among the guilty.

Day 2
That Ole Swing

My initial training for being a pastor was experience. Son of a pastor, being in church all my life, a college degree, and having preached revivals and taught Bible classes for about ten years were my printable credentials. A Calling and prayer were between my heart and the Master.

Oh, there was one thing more. I had fancy notions of going into the FBI [already taken the entrance test with high marks] when Laila convinced me to talk to the Bishop about the possibility of pastoring a church. I was the most surprised when a few days later we were committed to a seemingly hopeless little group of people in a more hopeless looking building on the worst side of a little town.

Nothing was easy. The town manager did not like Pentecostals. He had openly remarked that Pentecostals should go out of town into the country where they belonged. Our church building was in the last section of the town to get rid of outdoor toilets. Our whole community was stigmatized. Forget rich folks attending our church. They would not even drive through our part of the town.

Mentoring was not a concept discussed in those days. It was not a familiar word. Pastors of hugely successful churches with sudden growth into the hundreds or thousands would hold conferences for other pastors. They were the heroes, i.e., the role models. Pastors of smaller churches paid fees to listen and try to take home materials they purchased. "Do what I do, and you will get the same results I get," was the general notion. Nothing could be further from the truth.

I like Dr. John Maxwell. Money spent to attend his conferences has been worthwhile. However, even after talking with Dr. Maxwell, shaking his hand, and being near him, I have not been able to remember names of parishioners like Dr. Maxwell. We are different. Haven't acquired his ability to remember names and faces of newcomers.

A day came in my young pastoral life when doubts were afflicting me as to whether it was time to acknowledge failure and move on. Maybe I was in the wrong place. Maybe the community was too hard for a good work for Jesus. Maybe I was not called to be a pastor.

In order to understand the rest of this story you must meet my Mother. She is of German descent. Tough as nails. Nine children. She has stood tall, supported her pastor husband, and marched on. She is good stock. One of her best traits is that she cannot and will not tolerate whining. Like as not a child coming to her to whine about some injustice on the playground might get a nice little whack on the bottom for whining. I once ran to her thinking my Brother Bradley would get what was coming to him: "Mama, Bradley threw a rock at me!"

"Did he hit you?" she asked without emotion.

"No, but the rock almost hit me," I indicted.

"A miss is as good as mile," she dismissed the matter.

I was a pastor facing challenges, and I had no legitimate place to share my burdens or doubts about my place in the

Kingdom. I lifted my chin and marched on as if all were well. Laila was my confidant. We talked, but agreed not to share our feelings and thoughts with anyone. We would just pray and keep working until the Lord made plain what to do, i.e., stay, leave, or whatever.

When I don't know what else to do as a pastor I make another visit, call a parishioner, or write a card of encouragement. Duty calls. A pastor goes. I was visiting. Up the walk I went to Sister Coley's home. It was an old frame house that had too long needed another coat of white paint. The steps were creaky, the wrap-around porch needed replacement boards, and the screen door sagged leaving holes that frustrated its purpose.

I raised my hand to knock on the screen door, but hesitated at the thought that this would make it bang. A loud noise came from inside the house. I listened. It was Sister Coley. She was praying.

She had diabetes, high blood pressure, heart trouble, bad knees and ears, and a stroke had twisted her jaw just enough to prevent wearing dentures. One side of her mouth had also been affected by the stroke.

When Sister Coley prayed, she prayed loud. When Sister Coley prayed, she had a routine. I did not know all this the day I stood on her porch with my hand raised to knock. I came to know.

"I cannot interrupt her prayer," I thought. "I will just stand here and wait until she is through before knocking." I waited. She prayed. Finally, I sat down in the rickety old swing on the porch. Surely it would not be too long.

She told God she loved him. She told God about the Mayor of the town, and all the councilmen. She prayed for each one of her eight children. Then she prayed for her church. She had helped to start the church during the Great Depression. In 1930 she paid 90 cents per week tithe out of her salary of $9.00 as a scrub woman for rich folks.

If I had been in a hurry, or if I was thinking about leaving, my attention was suddenly arrested. Sister Coley began to tell God about her pastor. She told God things that I thought were secret. She told God that I was "discouraged." That woman must have been reading my mail, and she told Jesus all about it. Then she told Jesus that she loved her pastor.

She seemed to be finishing when I rose up from the swing. I did not knock on the door. I did stop at the top of the stairs. I shook myself, spiritually. I kicked myself in the rear, mentally. I talked to myself, quietly.

"Pastor, if an old woman can live on Social Security in an old frame house and pray for you, get your chin up and stop whining."

I never told Sister Coley how her prayer that day changed my life and brought contentment to me. When God appoints a pastor, He knows what He is doing. I thank God for That Ole Swing.

Day 3
Hank Snow

The snow was approaching a foot deep. At that time the church still owned the big Blue Goose bus, which was the only method of transportation in such weather. Town had shut down. Streets were not plowed. Nothing was moving, except me in the Blue Goose that seemed to love the snow both uphill and down.

Harold, a friend of mine, was a former alcoholic, now saved and sober, doing lay ministry. He owned a downtown restaurant. His was the only business open on Main Street. He had cooked a pot of soup, just in case a customer would come.

We sat talking. The snow kept coming. The phone rang. He talked intensely. I gathered there was a problem.

Hanging up the phone he said to me: "You will have to go. I will come later. Clyde is drunk again and threatening to kill his mother, sister, and burn the house down. You go, and I will come just as soon as I can turn stoves off and close."

Here was my opportunity to be Sir Galahad on a snowy day. I arrived at the little frame house on a side street and parked the Blue Goose. Before arriving at the door I could hear the sounds of violence and profanities.

The door opened and I found myself immediately in the middle of an impossible situation. Clyde was not only drunk, he was tall and had arms longer than an octopus. His sister was mentally ill, off her medicine, and screaming—more like shrieking! Clyde's mother weighed about 90 pounds and with a wailing voice was pleading with him not to set the house on fire.

In a three-ring circus, I made a quick decision that Clyde was the most dangerous. Catching him off guard I thrust my palm against his chest and sent him falling back into a foam futon. My calculations were correct. He was too drunk to get up. Oh, but he did give me a good cussing that I did not think I deserved.

"Mama," he shouted, "get me the rifle. I am going to shoot this preacher!"

"Son," she shrieked, "it is not nice to shoot preachers!"

"Ma'am, leave that gun where it is. I happen to agree with you that it is not nice to shoot preachers," I said firmly.

My confidence was that Harold would be along any minute to join me in helping to resolve the situation. He did not come. I turned a footstool up on its end and sat above Clyde, but out of reach of those long arms trying to flail me into pulp. Each time he started to get up I would watch carefully and thrust my palm again to his chest, knocking him off balance and back to the futon. Each of these experiences only added additional words to his vocabulary about his low opinion of me and his intent to speed me on the way to my Maker.

I started the experience with the best of religious intentions. Prayer and scripture filled my heart and mind. I quoted all the scripture I could remember. I prayed fervently. I foolishly tried reasoning. Finally, I talked. I talked until I told all I knew. Then I told Clyde about Christmas and Santa Claus, snow…nothing worked. The nightmare continued.

Day Three

In a moment of desperation I doubted that Harold had ever been my friend. Certainly in this moment friendship was being tested. I concluded that I deserved the title of "The Most Stupid Man in Wythe County." I could have been home with Laila and the children, sitting by the fire, drinking hot chocolate, and looking out at the wonder of the snow. Instead, the Blue Goose had ridden me into trouble. I would sell the Blue Goose.

"What can I do?" I exclaimed as I shoved him backwards one more time amidst another stream of vindictives.

"Sing," he said.

"Sing," I thought. "This is insane. I am in a house of mentally ill people and a drunk wants me to sing." But I reasoned that if he said "Sing" it might work. Nothing else had worked. Try.

I sang the first verse of Amazing Grace to more shrieks and screams, but Clyde settled back. I thought to myself: "This is the craziest thing I have ever done." I decided to sing the second verse.

Well, Clyde seemed to relax a little more. I thought to myself, "You know there is no one here to remember with any sanity this experience except me. I feel pretty good about my singing." Sitting even more erect on the footstool, but keeping a good eye on Clyde, I took a deep breath and began the third verse.

Clyde went to flailing those long arms again. I thought the battle was starting all over. "Hold it right there!" He said as if directing a choir. I stopped singing, wondering what was next. He continued by jamming a finger in my direction, "You think you are Hank Snow, don't you?" I had to laugh at his reference to the popular country singer who sold more than 80 million records during his career.

Well, the police came. They took Clyde to thaw out. No charges in those days, just a friendly thawing out. When they marched him down the walk in the still falling snow his mother yelled to the daughter: "Get me a butcher knife. I am going to slit that preacher's throat."

But I was already on my way to the Blue Goose. I made my way home to Laila and the children. My recitation of the day's events was met with no sympathy. Worst part was Laila laughed at me and said: "You just had to do what no one else was doing and go to town, didn't you?"

When things have cooled off and down, often a pastor can look back and imagine that God was also laughing. Who knows, maybe He did make my voice sound like Hank Snow's for just a short time!

Day 4
The Auction

Substitute teaching in high school brought in about $30 per day. That was a bonus to my small and unstable paycheck—only a percentage of the weekly offering. The west side of the school where I substituted faced the side of a high hill across the road from the only local golf course. An old farmhouse and falling down barn told stories of better times.

"That would be a wonderful place for a church," I would think to myself as I stood looking out the window of the high school. I was daydreaming. Land for a church across from a golf course? Then one day I passed by the ole farm and saw an auction sign. The land had been divided into lots of an acre each.

"What if two lots could be purchased for a new church location?" I mused. An emergency meeting was called of the few members. I suggested that we borrow up to $15,000 to bid at the auction. Another person shockingly suggested $25,000. When the question was asked where we would get that much money, one dear elderly parishioner spoke out, "Rob a bank." There was laughter.

Incredibly, a local banker that I knew gave me a letter assuring that he would underwrite a $25,000 loan. A committee of three men and the pastor went to the auction. The church was the highest bidder for two lots. Later in the day the auctioneer blocked five lots and a 14-acre tract. The bid price for each was added plus 10%. The starting price was $41,000.

The church committee recognized we had no authority to bid. However, the four of us retreated, formed a partnership, shook hands, and went in to bid personally. By agreement one was to start. From different points in the large gathering another would pick up the bid if it rose. Finally, I would come in at $46,000. When I came into the bidding there were three millionaires and a preacher left. Two millionaires realized my intent for a new church on the property and ceased to bid.

The auctioneer later declared that he speeded through his language to say: "One. Twice. Three times. Sold!" to the Reverend.

It was a court-ordered sale. Cash. The old lawyer handling the estate matter for the court set up office on the porch of the old house. The loudspeaker boomed my name to come and settle the account. I represented the largest purchase of the day, an impressive amount of money at that time!

There I stood without the expected certified check, but with a letter indicating the willingness of a bank to loan the church $25,000. Somehow I talked my way into signing a paper and promising the lawyer I would bring money to his office on Monday.

Oh, it was a long weekend. I was so sure that I could find another $25,000, which would include closing costs. Most of Monday passed and no bank could promise $50,000 without a board meeting.

Monday afternoon I met the Clerk of the church as he returned home from work. We rushed to the bank and personally borrowed $5,000 with both of us on a signature note. Taking a

Day Four

check I went to the lawyer's office. I knew his secretary to be a nice lady. "Do you want to speak to the lawyer?" she asked.

"Oh, no. Thank you," I assured her. "I just need a receipt for this check for $5,000." With the receipt in hand I hastened down the hallway and into a waiting car. With intent I stayed away from a phone until the next morning. This was in pre-cell phone days.

"Reverend Bare, I received your check for $5,000, but it is a little short," he began. The dreaded call had come.

"Mr. Parsons," I said, "Am I to think that you are pushing me?"

"Well," he responded, "you know this is a court ordered sale."

"Mr. Parsons, is 10% not a legal down payment in the Commonwealth of Virginia?" I continued.

"Well, now," he seemed to muse, "I reckon you do have a point."

Feeling pretty good about having said something I did not know to be a fact, I pressed on: "And another thing. We want a title search before making any further payment," I asserted. As if I knew what I was talking about, which I did not.

"You do have that right," he said. "We will get it done."

When the title search was done Mr. Parsons explained to me that if we had paid for the property in full and taken title on the day of sale an additional debt of some $16,000 for a past judgment would have been ours.

In time the church bought all the land that the four of us personally purchased. A beautiful new sanctuary was built on the prime piece of property.

Did not Jesus promise that the Holy Spirit would lead and guide into all truth? The Holy Spirit not only knows about the laws of God. The Holy Spirit knows about man's laws. The Holy Spirit is available to all, even a scared preacher!

Day 5
God Told Me

Sister Kegley was an elderly widow of a Methodist pastor. She came to our parish. It was a mutual love affair.

She came faithfully. Though she had been the wife of a pastor, there was never a sense of judgment or comparison. She was an encourager.

The first phase of our building program was nearing completion. Interest rates were high. Money was tight. We did not have a construction loan. About $10,000 was owed to local building suppliers. They needed their money. We had no money.

"Pastor, I would like for you to bring Laila and Danny and Dana and come to my home for dinner," she said. The idea of going to the country for a wonderful meal was delightful. She was an outstanding cook! We accepted.

Dessert completed, Sister Kegley said matter-of-factly, "Let us move out to the patio and talk."

She came directly to the point. "The Lord spoke to me that I am to borrow $10,000 on a First Deed of Trust against my home."

That was a frightful proposition. Her home was debt-free. What would people think of a young pastor letting a Methodist minister's widow mortgage her home? It would be the talk of the community. I resisted.

"I want you to take me to the bank," she continued. "Now, we will go tomorrow. I know what the Lord has said."

We did go to the bank. Then she insisted that I go with her into the bank and talk with the president, who was a long-time personal friend of her family. My position was most uncomfortable as the president of the bank did everything he could do to convince Sister Kegley not to borrow money and loan it to anyone. Anyone, I knew, included the young preacher sitting beside her. He did not speak it out loud, but he made clear to her that disaster could come if she persisted in making the loan.

"I know when the Lord speaks to me," she spoke to the banker. "The Lord spoke to me. I realize that you are a family friend, and I appreciate your advice. However, if you refuse to make the loan I will go to the other bank down the street. They also know me and will loan the money," she said firmly.

We walked out with a check for $10,000. We were able to continue construction and to pay all bills on time. Before the note was due I took a check for $10,000 plus interest and all fees and went to the bank. It was a moment of personal gratification to place the check into the hands of the president and make sure all documents were satisfactorily released. I will never forget that feeling.

Time passed and there was the need for $200,000 for another building program. I remembered the widow and the bank.

Time passed and there was the need for $2,000,000 for yet another building program. I remembered the widow and the bank.

Day Five

God is faithful! Though dollar amounts have often been larger, I can truthfully say that no financial need I have faced as a pastor in the last 30 years has been bigger than the $10,000 provided by a Methodist minister's widow. It was a victory that yet speaks of God's sovereign provision.

Day 6
Having Church

Danny and Dana came along to delight our hearts and home. Laila got what she wanted, a boy first and then a girl. Danny is just two months short of being two years older than Dana.

Danny was ever the child to be careful. We called him "Grandpa Miller" after his maternal great-grandfather. He would not ride in swings over water. Little things I wanted us to do as father and son were often resisted by Danny as being "too dangerous."

If he was Mr. Safe, he was also Mr. Conservative. He really loved Jesus, and wanted to do everything just right. Laila and I often had to remind him that he was entitled to a childhood, i.e., he did not have to be grown-up before he was ten years old.

Once Laila found Danny and Dana in the little sanctuary that was our first pastoral assignment. Quietly, Laila observed as seven year-old Danny fervently preached to his five year-old sister. Dana was the sum total of his congregation.

As Danny preached Dana decided she would be happy and praise the Lord. She was in front of the pulpit jumping up and down and having herself a delightful time of celebrating Jesus' joy. Danny kept preaching.

Suddenly, Danny stopped. "Now, sister, you just sit down right now," he said. "You know that you cannot be up shouting with shorts on!"

To say the least Laila had her hands full moderating the dispute between Preacher Danny and Sister Dana. Dana had a divine right, in her opinion, and the Lord did not care if she had shorts on. But to Danny, it was a serious breach of proper dress in God's House. Dana should be more respectful. And, besides, who was she to question the Man of God?

Only after Danny and Dana were grown did Laila and I share with them how much we laughed over their Preacher Danny and Sister Dana episode. It is one of the best stories we have of our children growing up.

Sundays can be a lot like Preacher Danny and Sister Dana. Mr. and Mrs. Judgment can come to church. Not much is right. A lot is wrong. If everyone would just listen, Mr. and Mrs. Judgment feel they could make the pastor a better preacher, the ushers more effective, the elders wiser, and the pastor's wife a better servant—among other things.

Among other things includes Mr. and Mrs. Judgment's opinion that "having church" is the Number One priority. The way to "have church" is clearly defined in their imagination, and all other methods lack any scriptural credibility. They do not see nor care about ministry to the community or the world. Their concern is to make sure that everyone dresses and acts in a manner they define.

I do not know where the expression of "having church" came from. What I do know is that the concept has done more harm than good. A pastor who cares about his people and congregation will focus on maturing disciples, not judging saints. A pastor who lives by the "having church" syndrome will go home lots of Sundays feeling a total failure.

A pastor who lovingly shares the Word and ministers care will have few Sundays to have the post-anointing blues and feel like reading classifieds for a new career option. More frequent will be the times of refreshment and contentment from having challenged and blessed the people of God.

Shout on Sister!

Day 7
Intellectual Capacity

In time I completed a Masters Degree from The College of William and Mary. My hope was to teach at the local community college. The pay would be so much better than substitute teaching.

The Dean of Instruction and I were friends. He wanted me on staff, especially since I would be willing to teach classes in factories, prisons, and other extension sites.

My application was submitted. Credentials were confirmed. The Dean indicated that I should be approved as an instructor before the next quarter of classes.

But I was not approved on schedule. In fact, the approval did not come. Weeks dragged on. It became apparent that something was wrong.

"Walter," I said one day as we were talking, "be candid with me. What is holding up my application? I know there is a need for instructors. Why am I not being approved?"

"Well, Harold," he drawled, "If you must know there is a struggle. Three persons must approve your application: The President, the Dean of Instruction, and the Finance Officer. The President and I are agreed that you would be an asset." He stopped.

And, I queried, "What is the question or reason why the third person will not agree?"

"Since you insist," Walter intoned, "the third person has asked the question: 'Do you really think that someone of Pastor Bare's religious persuasion has the mental capability to teach on the college level?' He seriously doubts that you have the intellectual capacity."

"But, Walter," I insisted, "that is ridiculous. I have a valid BA from an accredited university. My MA is from one of the finest and most distinguished colleges in the world. I have taught public school three years and taught numerous college-level courses. In addition, I have valid non-ministry credentials. What is the question?"

"Harold, you do not understand. All that you say is true. However, you are a Pentecostal. He is prejudiced. He believes that anyone who is Pentecostal is mentally deficient. It is a battle we must wage. Be patient."

Walter and patience won out. I was given the opportunity to teach. In time I was the highest paid adjunct instructor of the local college.

The process of gaining acceptance was good for me. It helped me to realize there are those who just naturally have the wrong opinion of preachers. Changing the minds of these prejudiced persons is difficult to impossible. Sometimes we win. Sometimes not.

If a pastor takes such battles as a personal affront, it can be demeaning and discouraging. Feelings of failure and rejection can plague one's psyche. Confrontations will be perceived where there is no cause for alarm or offense.

Day Seven

It is good when a pastor knows Who called, and knows that the Calling is sure. It is good when a pastor feels secure in that Calling, regardless of what others think of the pastor's intellectual capacity.

Day 8
Competition

Preachers are human. While rejoicing for all things good, it is sometimes difficult not to feel a little envious when the nearest pastor's cathedral not only has a taller spire, but chimes. The *coup d'etat* is after a building program and borrowing a lot of money another pastor tells about building his cathedral debt-free. "God really blessed us," the other pastor says.

I am Pentecostal. Pentecostals are reputed for their preaching and long services. One of the closest neighbors to our church was an Episcopal church. One Sunday evening we had a wonderful worship service. By the time we were leaving almost two hours had passed.

Driving by the Episcopal church I was chagrined to discover that the parking lot was still full. Not a person was outside. This could only mean that the Episcopalians were still in worship.

Being Pentecostal and with much emphasis on Spirit-filled services, it was incomprehensible to me that the liturgy of Episcopalians could be producing longer worship services. While it is not standard form to compare Pentecostals to

Episcopalians, the fact was that the Episcopal pastor had come to his charge only months after my assignment. Both of us had the same first name. Both of us were making lots of changes. Both of us were attracting the attention of the larger community.

I drove on toward home, maybe a little more slowly. Laila and I talked about the full parking lot of the Episcopalians.

It was not until a few weeks later that we learned the Episcopal church was an officially designated site for a chapter of Alcoholics Anonymous. They met there on Sunday nights. Most of the attendees were present by court order.

The other Harold had perhaps been home in bed or out fishing, while I had been feeling twinges of envy that Episcopalians might be having longer worship services than Pentecostals!

Laughter was spontaneous. My humanity had met me full circle. Behind all the religious rhetoric and piety, the pastor is still a person. And people just naturally feel the pressure of peers.

Isn't there a Scripture that says something about not being wise when we compare ourselves.......[II Cor. 10:12].

Day 9
Change

There is a clear line of division in ministry. Many think that a new pastor should make no changes for maybe the first six months. Others believe that a new pastor should make changes as quickly as possibly in a non-threatening way.

I loved and admired the former pastor. We were friends. He had served the church as its founding pastor for a total of 22 years. I agreed to keep him on staff until the next phase of the building program was completed and his social security payments began. While I felt change was important, I wanted to respect and not offend him.

What could I change? We were in a temporary worship area, so we decided to begin there. First, the pulpit area was moved from the corner to the middle of the longest side of the room. Second week a platform was built for the pulpit. Third week we hung fabric on the wall behind the pulpit to give a softer effect than painted block.

Folks liked each change. There was no protest. The objective was to make a change that would be visible before people sat down for worship.

Some things just grow. The initial idea had no seeds of any long-range plan. The idea led to an action. As action was repeated each week, in time there was a sense of continuity. A plan evolved.

I do not remember when but it came to my consciousness that it would be good to make a change every week for the first year. I looked for change that did not cost much and did not require any meetings or discussions. Sometimes it was as simple as a potted plant being placed on the organ.

How I wish I had kept a list of things done week to week. There was never a complaint. Never a protest. Seemed like folks got to the point of expectation—looking for what was different, kind of like little kids' sheets in a restaurant asking "Can you find seven objects in this picture?"

About Week 32 I ran out of ideas. It was Saturday. Sunday was coming. Nothing came to mind. Finally, in an act of desperation I picked up a shovel and dug a hole in the grass beside the front door. Nice little pile of dirt. Then I stuck the shovel in the top of the pile of dirt.

Sunday came. Folks came down the sidewalk. There was the pile of dirt and the shovel. "Pastor," someone asked, "What is this?"

Nonchalantly as I could muster I replied, "Oh, someone is donating a nice shrub to be planted there. But they did not have time to get it in the ground before Sunday."

No one knew that I was the one buying the shrub. They just knew another change was in process. Folks just nodded and walked on in to worship.

Fifty-two weeks with a change each Sunday was completed. I never told the congregation that this was a goal I had set for us. Some will know it for the first time when they read this story.

Day Nine

The results of changing little things each week for 52 Sundays have been wonderful. Our congregation is accepting of change. We have never had a division over building. Projects of significance are advanced, put into action, and completed without so much as a ripple in the congregation. Remodeling programs are assumed to be part of general church operation, not a time for bickering and committee fussing.

Of this I am sure, pastors do well to study change. Most of what we do is technique. While doctrine is unchangeable, techniques change with the times. If a congregation can buy into the need for change it will be a great factor in happiness for the pastor and the people.

Day 10
Tom

Tom was my friend. He came to church when he came to church, if you know what I mean. You never knew when he would come. He would never promise to come. But you knew that if he died or needed a preacher it would be you.

He was a tree trimmer and woods person—strong as an ox. Up a tree he could go with whatever tools it took to get the job done. As he went up he would be spitting a steady stream of tobacco and talking to himself in language not learned in Sunday School.

Tom had a problem. He was supposed to be taking medicine to help keep his mind in balance. Sure as shooting, if Tom forgot to take his medicine, he got out of balance.

But, whether Tom came to church or not, he always respected me. Always came to help me if I needed help.

One day he was trimming a tree for my mother-in-law. It was a very high poplar on top of a steep embankment. About 25 feet up in the tree, Tom's chainsaw quit. He braced off and jerked the cord multiple times in an attempt to crank the saw. I stood back at a safe distance, not to be protected from the limbs, but to be out of reach of the steady stream of tobacco juice he spit with vengeance. The madder he got, the more he would spit. Then the cussing started.

Suddenly, without warning, Tom hurled the chainsaw down through the limbs. It bounced on the ground and rolled down the embankment to the road below. Down the tree he came. Stomping down to the road he picked up the chainsaw and once more pulled the string. "Can you believe the dad-blamed [family-friendly version of the words he used] thing won't work?" he exclaimed.

I laughed and said: "What did you expect, Tom, after a mule's arm threw it 40 feet?"

There was another time I needed Tom. Rumor had it that Tom was seeing a woman whose reputation was not sterling. Not being able to reach Tom by phone I asked his mother where the home of the woman was.

It was early morning and very cold when I knocked on the door. A boy about 7 years old answered. He was one of four or five children in the home, each maybe by a different father.

"Is Tom here," I asked.

"Yeah, Preacher. He's in there. Just go on in," the boy said.

I opened the door and stepped into the room. The other children were gathered around an old wood stove, almost ready to hug the warmth out of it, or so it seemed. Tom was lying in bed beside the woman with his hand generously into the top covering her bosom.

There was silence for what seemed like an eternity and Tom spoke with rebuke in his voice: "Preacher," he drawled, "I know what you are thinking, but you just have a dirty mind."

Well, by now you get the idea.

Day Ten

Tom souped up his old truck. Did I tell you that he was a super mechanic? That old sixwheel truck would "mortally fly," as country boys would say. One night Tom heard voices telling him to go see a friend about ten miles away. He went off the interstate and up the ramp at 110 mph. So? Well, halfway up the ramp he decided to take a shortcut. He turned off the pavement and across the grass. The truck hit an embankment, went airborne, landed in the second part of the four-lane road above and smashed the side of the bridge.

When the ambulance came Tom sat in his truck bleeding and cussing. He told the medics that he would kill any person who put their hands on him. Finally, he agreed that if they would back off he would get out of his truck and lie down on the stretcher. They did. He did.

I arrived at the hospital about 2 AM. He had been treated and put in bed. I knew the doctors and whispered to them that Tom should be straitjacketed. Doing so, they scoffed at the idea and reminded me that he had hit a wall at more than 100 mph.

Well, with things settling down I decided to go home and get some rest. Tom was going to live, or so it appeared.

"Tom," I said, "I am going home to get some rest. Do you want me to pray with you before I go?

"I don't need prayer," he said curtly, but not disrespectfully. "I am God."

"Tom," I replied, "you are not only not God, you are in a hospital bed with a straitjacket, and you cannot get up unless others help you."

He was silent for a moment and then kindly said: "You are right, Preacher. Let's pray."

A little later Tom was found going down the hallway—out of the straitjacket.

A pastor's life can be so colorful, so full of experiences, and mixed with successes and failures. God does not fail, but sometimes a pastor is not able to reach even a friend for Jesus. It is so painful.

There is a Tom in every pastor's life.

Day 11
Never On A Sunday

Folks humorously comment, though the humor cannot always be detected, that pastors only work one day each week. Of course the implication is that all a pastor does is preach on Sundays. I never laugh at the intended joke. It is one I find dry of humor and wisdom.

Laila was an only child. On Saturdays she and her mom cleaned house until 12 noon. With both hands on the clock straight up, they changed clothes to go to town looking and shopping. Papa Baggett said they only came home when the stores closed. The evening was filled with Laila and her mom playing games, laughing, and watching Gunsmoke. Her dad, a pastor, was doing what I do. Marrying a pastor was not Laila's intent. She knew what a pastor did on Saturday night.

Sunday begins on Saturday for me. Laila sometimes says the most lonely night of the week for her is Saturday night. Her husband, a pastor for 30 years, begins to withdraw. No party spirit. Wants to be home. Wants quiet. Wants to go to bed early and take with him a pile of books. She often tiptoes into the room to find her pillow long after her husband is sleeping.

Sunday follows Saturday. It took some time serving as a pastor before Laila and I came upon a necessary covenant. There was one thing we agreed that we would NOT do on a Sunday. We knew that doing that one thing on a Sunday could distract me, cause me to lose focus, and maybe do or say something, or not do or not say something, that would be inconsistent with my duties as a pastor.

Laila and I agreed that never on a Sunday would she raise issues that could be delayed until Monday. There, now you have a family secret. She is a wise woman who understands that our closeness and shared life could be used to disrupt what the Holy Spirit seeks to do through a pastor on Sunday.

Be patient. I will tell you the rest: I do not always look forward to Mondays. She is not harsh, not unkind, but she does not wrap truth up in candy packages. She says she married a strong man, and a strong man should take his own medicine. She says if I am going to speak plainly to others, then I should take my medicine without complaining.

When Laila decides to do what we agreed not to do on a Sunday it is always private. If she says, "Can we go for a ride," it may be a clue. If she says, "Can we talk?" or to the grandchildren after dinner, "Go out and play. Papa and I are going to talk," it may be a clue.

Lest you misunderstand, it is not her intent to bring me down. She does not approach the conversation in the spirit of "Bubba, let me help you to understand that I am as smart as you" though she is. She may begin by saying, "I want you to think about," or "Don't be upset, but we need to discuss," or "I want you to know I love you, and I think you are a better person than what you said," or in the event I have become discouraged she may say, "The man I love is capable of more."

Day Eleven

What I do know is that Sundays are primetime for a pastor. Adrenalin is pumping. All the senses are keenly attuned to serve. A good wife who cooperates with the work of the Holy Spirit will surely have a great reward on earth and in heaven. A great service is done when she shares points for improvement lovingly on a Monday. But never on a Sunday!

Day 12
The Lawyer

Oh how we needed to buy land and relocate the church. We could not add any building to our tiny parcel of land. Our congregation had grown from 17 the first Sunday. We had added an office and five classrooms to our one-room-only sanctuary, but more space was needed.

Congregations do not tend to go where the pastor does not lead. A pastor is so much more than a sermon on Sunday. It gradually dawned on me that someone needed to look for land. Thus, my movement about the little town began to have a secondary motive: I was always looking for land that would be appropriate for a church relocation. Inquiries were made without success.

When I saw that six acres on a nice knoll, my heart leaped. It was vacant, thus no need to demolish any buildings. It was in a good section of the town. Access roads were good.

A legal search gave knowledge that the land's owner was a state politician, perhaps the most powerful lawyer in town. Excitement gripped my heart with hope. An appointment was made to visit with him.

In his law office I shared interest in buying his land for a relocation of the church. He leaned back and said: "Well, let's have an understanding. I am a politician. You are a preacher. I need you to understand that it would not be a good turn in the community for there to be a question about business relations between me and a local church. Therefore, when I tell you the price, I am asking you to accept that as the final price. The land is for sale, but there can be no negotiations over the price I give you. Is that clear?"

There was little choice but to accept his terms. In my heart I was hoping for a number that was so reasonable it would need no negotiation. The price he stated was so outrageous that I was shocked. Only he and the Lord know whether I kept my composure.

Anger burned inside me. I wanted to think it was righteous anger. Thoughts filled my head with words that I wanted him to hear about his greed, his manipulation, and his callousness.

Instead, I stood up politely, reached to shake his hand, and said: "Thank you very much for the discussion. However, I can assure you that the price is beyond our capability as a congregation."

It seemed he was a little surprised by the quick closure. He shook my hand and said: "Well, if there is ever anything I can do for you or the congregation please let me know."

Down those wooden stairs I dejectedly walked. I wanted the echo to be a sound of protest that would bring guilt to his heart. Instead, I left as quietly as I could.

Many, many Sundays later land had been found. A new sanctuary had been erected. A new day seemed to be dawning for our congregation. We were no longer fledgling. We were flying. Our

Day Twelve

outreach was not only community, but we were also involved in mission work across the United States and in other countries.

At a critical moment of transition from the old property to the new property the church came upon a legal tangle that could have been a devastating setback. A lawyer was needed immediately to negotiate a delicate matter. I remembered the promise of the politician/lawyer to help if there was ever a need.

Better yet, he remembered his promise. The church's legal needs were made a priority. Issues were resolved. His total bill for services was $60!

Many times I have wondered what could have been the fall-out if I had responded to the lawyer in anger over his absurd price for land. I have more often wondered that the Holy Spirit is able to override human impulses for the benefit of Christ's glory and the good of the Church.

A pastor must learn to walk humbly even when human feelings and emotions are sounding loudly on the inside.

Day 13
Methodist Neighbor

One could not have asked for a better neighbor. She was quiet, decent, church-going, loved our children, and would even share a dessert, if we came to get it.

Don't remember her ever coming into our yard. We were Pentecostal. She had a thing about Pentecostals, like she was afraid of them. So long as we did not ask her to church or talk about our religious beliefs with her, all was well.

One morning about four AM I awoke with a start. Rest assured, I work hard for Jesus. When I go to bed I virtually die until at least six hours have passed. My faith in the Resurrection is renewed each morning. But this night I awoke far too early with a start.

Being a slow learner, it took me some time following Jesus to learn that the Spirit often likes to speak in the quietest hours of the night. More than once I have proffered that it would be more agreeable to me if the Holy Spirit would allow me to finish my sleep before wanting to open office to discuss business. The discussion always comes out the same. I lose.

So I was awake. Out on my knees I went beside the bed. "Lord," I said matter-of-factly but politely, "it would mean a lot to me if you would just get to the point. Tell me what is on your mind so I can go back to sleep."

Clear as a bell, a voice spoke into the silent darkness. "Your neighbor in the hospital will have emergency surgery. She will have untreatable cancer."

Shaking my head at such a message I crawled back into bed. About six AM I nudged Laila. "I must share something with you." I said. "In case it happens I want a witness."

It came to pass just as the voice had whispered to me that morning. I thought to myself, "So what is the big deal with God waking me up with that message."

Being neighbors the only proper thing to do was to visit the hospital, though I knew that she would not want me to act as a pastor. It was a difficult day for her. She began to tell the bad news and ending up turning her back to me and sobbing into her pillow.

Not knowing what to do I patiently waited. Finally, she seemed to calm down. I said: "Can I share something with you?" She nodded yes. Then I told her about my being awakened at four in the morning. I shared with her what the Lord had impressed in my heart.

She listened. I could not think of what else to say. There was silence. Then I continued: "Here is what I think. If the Lord awakened me to tell me about you when I am not your pastor, He must really love you. I know He loves me. He would not take sleep from me without good reason. He wants me to tell you that He was thinking about you. He cares for you. He loves you."

That day a Methodist who did not like Pentecostals had a change of heart. She rose to greater faith as we shared prayer.

Day Thirteen

Though the doctors only gave her a few months to live, she lived several years. His ways are so different from our ways! Praise Him!

Day 14
Oh SO Smart

We were not long at the new parish when the idea of a revival surfaced. "Why not put up posters in unusual public places?" I thought to myself. This of course led to the obvious: "What places would be unusual for a revival poster?"

A journey was made through the town to search out display areas. Returning home it occurred to me that the Silver Diner Saloon would be just such a place. Back out I went. I pulled to the front of the diner and hesitated. My picture being in the paper with a weekly news article, my face and role as a pastor was commonly known.

The diner was like a mobile home with windows the full length of the front. The door was in the center. The cash register was directly in front of the door. I stepped directly to the cash register, carrying with me posters and tape.

From the outside I had seen booths occupied with men. Stepping through the door peripheral vision had made me aware of cards, money, and beer on every table.

"May I help you?" the waitress politely asked.

"Would you mind if I put up a revival poster?" I directed my remark to her without turning my head or looking around.

"Sure," she said. When I asked where, she said, "Wherever you like!" and her tone sounded a note of gladness.

The front of the cash register seemed a good place to me. I took my time. Made sure it was lined up just perfectly and precision taped. Every person entering would see it first. I thanked her and turned to leave.

"Hey, Reverend, could you answer a Bible question?" I heard a voice. Pausing, I slowly looked around. To my surprise not a table had beer, cards, or money. Men were just sitting with folded hands looking at each other.

"I suppose so," I respectfully said. Thereupon, a question was asked about the Battle of Armageddon.

For some twenty minutes I was a fountain of wisdom and knowledge. Whatever they asked I was able to answer and take them further into the mysteries of prophecies of things to come. They were awed. My performance was stellar. I never felt as good in a college classroom. I imagined revival beginning right there in that saloon. They would all be saved. The whole town would hear. It was wonderful!

How we brought the question and answer time to a close I do not remember. I do remember walking out the door feeling very scholarly. I could hardly wait to get home and tell Laila what had happened. It was a story worth telling and writing.

Just out the door I happened to turn in such a way as to see through the windows. Even as I looked the cards, money and beer were coming back to the table. Nothing had changed.

I drove away feeling very foolish. Pastors learn that it is unwise to give meat to babies. It is difficult to lead people to Christ

Day Fourteen

with stories about Armageddon, Gog and Magog, the anti-christ, the mark of the beast, and battles in the Valley of Megiddo.

Though the esoteric and titillating may stir the mind, the heart needs to hear the simple message of Jesus come to seek and to save that which is lost. I decided that day to never teach prophecy to unbelievers. To use one's intellect and knowledge in an effort to impress others is vain and foolish.

Simple is the gospel. Much is the need for it.

Day 15
Jerry

He came to us as an associate. He and his good wife were a God-sent blessing.

Our congregation was growing, but finances were tight. A lot of volunteer work had to be done by parishioners and staff. There are two sides to volunteer work in a congregation. While it can be necessary because of finances, it also can be healthy as an outlet for energies and in building *esprit de corp*. The need in regard to finances was obvious. We did gain a lot of momentum from shared experiences of volunteer work.

Our new sanctuary needed the outside trim painted near the roof. Jerry, faithful and willing, set himself the task of painting the highest part. It was about 20 feet above the sidewalk. He was not a professional painter. While he was at the top of the ladder the feet of the ladder on the hard surface below began to slide. It was all too quick. Jerry landed with ladder, bucket and paint on the concrete with a crash.

He was not unconscious, but they knew he was badly hurt. A young teenage boy was inside a classroom and heard the noise. He rushed out to investigate. There Jerry lay in the mess of paint, critically injured, yet conscious.

The boy was in shock.

"Call the emergency number and get an ambulance," Jerry said.

The boy took off back into the church without saying a word. Then he burst back out the door panting for air and gasping: "What is the number for 911?"

Jerry is witty. "Try 911," he wryly said, and to this day he laughs about that teenage boy asking for the telephone number.

The worst of Jerry's injuries was that wrists and elbows were crushed. He ended up in the hospital with both arms suspended and surgery being a must. But he was alive, and for this we praised the Lord.

When church service was over the following Sunday night some of us went to visit Jerry in the hospital. I took his ministerial Ordination Certificate that we had planned to present to him with ceremony in worship Sunday morning. Instead, we would honor him and present the certificate in the hospital. It was a hallowed moment. He was deeply moved.

A crisis developed. Pain increased. The nurse sent for a doctor. The doctor determined that swelling was pressing against nerves in his wrists. Immediate surgery would be required to prevent permanent paralysis in his hands.

By now it was 10 PM. The surgery would be done by a resident. This I did not want. One of the finest sports surgeons in the world was part of the staff. I knew the surgeon's wife through academic connections. He had agreed to take Jerry's case upon my personal request.

But surgery had to be NOW! The doctor on duty informed us that it would take a few minutes to get a team together. He left.

Day Fifteen

We prayed. When we had finished praying, Jerry did the unthinkable. He pressed his arms upward lifting them above the medical slings. "Lord," Jerry prayed, "These are your arms and hands. You can do with them what you want to." He then spoke in Spirit language between himself and his Heavenly Father as the arms rested.

"Now," the nurse said with urgency, "we must go."

"Would you please ask the doctor to come back," Jerry asked.

When the doctor came in Jerry calmly said: "Doctor, I know that it may be unusual. But would you please check my hands one more time?"

An astonished doctor declared that the swelling had gone down, the emergency was over, and surgery could be postponed.

Jerry and Kathy pastor a church in Pennsylvania. They are doing a wonderful ministry of reaching a community. He has use of his arms and hands. He is still witty.

There are mysteries to this calling of being a pastor. Why does God sometimes heal a person partly, but not wholly? Why do good people get hurt doing godly ministry? There are other questions I have as a pastor. I ease the pressure for answering such questions by remembering the faith of people like Jerry, who in the face of adversity recognize God is a sovereign God. I am an under-shepherd. Christ is the Chief Shepherd.

Day 16
A Visit to a Factory

On a visit home from college, I was spending time with my Dad. He was a pastor. The duties of a pastor are never completed.

Dad asked if I minded stopping by a local factory that made products that could be obtained by non-profit organizations, including churches, for resale.

"You can go into the factory with me," he said. "I just need to look at some items and talk to one of our church ladies who works in the factory."

My intellectual world was challenged to return to the real world of people as I walked through different sections. It is so easy for a college student to think the whole world is about classrooms and degrees, titles and positions.

In reality, only about 4% of the world's population has a college degree, with a much smaller percentage of graduate degrees. The high school drop-out rate in the United States is still almost 25%.

A walk through many factories and work areas is a painful reality. Persons work long hours for wages that insure sustenance living. Work with hands and feet are more fundamental than requirements for education.

In the back corner Dad and I found the Clerk of the parish. She was a faithful woman. She greeted her pastor with respect and good cheer. Dad introduced me. I stood quietly observing and listening.

They talked about the products. As an employee she would be able to obtain products at a discount, which would help with a church fund-raising project.

My mind was captured more with the scenario. Dad had told me that the Clerk had worked in this factory and this same room for many years. He said she was one of the best members of the parish, faithful in attendance, helpful with ministries, and devoted to tithing and giving.

I pondered about the woman. What could cause her such good cheer? How could she be so pleasant in such a dismal place? What would be her future? Would she grow old and retire in this work place?

Paint had lost its luster. The floor was concrete. Noise of machines and motion of boxes and products was incessant. No music. Lighting was basic factory lighting. No windows.

Then I noticed her legs below her modest dress. Varicose veins seemed almost as large as my little finger. I was stunned by the sight of those protruding vessels!

Later I asked Mom what could cause such varicose veins. Mom shared that standing long hours on a cold concrete floor probably had contributed to the problem.

It has been about 40 years since my visit to the factory where I saw those varicose veins. The memory is rich with me. Few things have impacted my life more dynamically than that visit with Dad to a factory.

Day Sixteen

Sunday comes in a pastor's life. There is a gathering of the saints. They have come from different walks of life. They bring their tithe and offerings.

In the factory that day long ago I came to reverence the hard work behind tithes and offerings. With my own eyes I saw the effort that dear and precious saints put into bringing home a paycheck that does not afford luxuries. Many have never been to a spa, never enjoyed a restaurant with linens and silver, never traveled to a foreign country, never flown in an airplane, and never been invited to the home of the wealthy or prestigious. What they have done is faithfully tithe.

They invested in their belief that the Church belongs to Christ. They invested in their belief that the pastor is called of God. They invested in missions and the work of the Lord with faith that one day they will sit at a table in heaven in the presence of Jesus.

They did not resent being good stewards. They did not complain. They trusted the pastor and leadership to manage tithes and offerings for the glory of Christ and His Church.

That saint with varicose veins in the factory so long ago did and does cause me to respect what stands behind tithes and offerings. No act of worship is higher.

Day 17
The Red Carpet

Our first pastorate was a tiny little church building that had 17 people come for the first service. Oh, the building was pitiful. About 24 by 36 square feet, it had a warped roof, unusable restrooms, and an ugly inside. It was down an embankment and had no classrooms. On top of that, a blackbird had nested in a crack of the outside wall and would set up an awful fuss any time during the service. How I sometimes grieved that my mother had taught me not to kill birds!

The people were good. Money was in short supply. The church mortgage was $87.84 monthly, and it was almost impossible to make the payment. We sold candy bars, hot dogs, chicken dinners, and apple pies to struggle along and complement the offerings.

No records exist to tell the painful story of painting, fixing up, adding classrooms, and trying to make things look better. While the progress was slow, it was measurable.

Then one night we held a business meeting. Forget all that stuff about boards and committees, elders and deacons. There was only a handful of us, and we were all in the boat together. We had borrowed $7,500, a frightful sum of money.

The congregation approved only after we got the terms extended and the payment lowered to $84.01 per month, less than the previous monthly payment.

Our discussion was general and very open. No formalities. We were just talking through what to do next.

Now you had to know Betsy to really appreciate her. She was an intelligent and wonderful lady married to careful and methodical Earl. Betsy just spoke her mind. It was her way. No pretense. No predication. Just Betsy.

"What do you suggest about carpet?" I asked. "Do you have a preference in color? The only thing that I would note to you is that we avoid red. Studies indicate that red causes boys to be more active." Enough said. I thought I was venturing pretty boldly into the conservative culture of rural southwestern Virginia.

There was silence. I thought for a moment maybe I had insinuated something that was being taken as an offense.

The silence was broken by Betsy: "Do you suppose we ought to put some red carpet in the old men's classroom?" she drawled as dry as last year's corn shucks.

To tell you the truth I cannot remember the rest of that meeting, or what happened after that. I was too stunned. Not offended, just surprised by Betsy's candid remark. I was more surprised that the good folks sensed the humor and there was healthy laughter.

A lot of Sundays have passed. I often think back to Betsy. She was an intervention in my life as a young pastor to remind me that people are people. Dress them up, put Sunday shoes on, send them to Oxford or Harvard, but in the end people are people. People marry. People have children. People have relationships with others. People have their quirks. People have their

Day Seventeen

esoteric behaviors. People are quiet. People are loud. People are introverts or extroverts.

Try as you might they cannot be pressed into one-size-fits-all. People are individuals. People have likes and dislikes. Women are women. Men are men. And, there are differences between the two.

Betsy was good for me. She helped me to understand that deep down inside of people, regardless of their age, they are human, vulnerable, and earthy. Sunday pews are filled with people.

Every pastor needs a parishioner like Betsy.

Day 18
Nightmare

The Sunday School teacher asked her teenage girls, "If you knew that you would die this week, what would you do?" Without a doubt they each had affirmed that making peace with Jesus would be the highest priority. Debbie, a 16-year-old, was the most adamant. The teacher prayed with them and later told me about their time of commitment.

Debbie was the daughter of a woman who worked a regular 40-hour job, but she also had a night and weekend job. Whether she got paid for the second job is not known to me. What is known is that the girls talked about sometimes having to sleep in the same room with mama and her whoever man. It was a dastardly thing to do on mama's part.

The one good virtue we could identify in Mama was that she allowed other folks to pick up her girls and take them to church. Of course, mama sometimes had to work her 40-hour job on weekends and this helped with baby-sitting. Mama never came to church. Church was not in her cards.

Friday came. Debbie had a boyfriend. They were out in his pick-up. Only God and the boyfriend know the rest of the story. What is known is that it began to snow. On a straight part of the country road the pick-up went off the pavement. The boy lost control. The vehicle rolled. Debbie went through the windshield.

Folks wondered whether Debbie may have told the boy that she was pregnant. He may have been less than happy with the announcement he was a daddy. She may have tried to jump from the vehicle, thus causing him to reach for her. The accident followed.

Whatever the truth, Debbie was prepared for burial without any tests or autopsy. Debbie was not a normal corpse. Going through the windshield had been a freakish accident. The glass cut off her entire face just in front of the ears and from under the chin to the top of her head. Morticians tried, but it was impossible to repair.

I went with Debbie's mama to the funeral home. We understood that the body was not presentable. The casket was sealed. We would weep over a closed casket with a spray on it and plan a memorial service for Debbie.

But mama got this thing in her head. She had to see her little girl one more time. Nothing the funeral directors could do could persuade mama to alter her course. It was her legal right: "Open it up. I don't care. I want to see my girl!" she demanded through her sobbing.

The directors did seem to move very slowly, protesting as they followed instructions. Finally the lid was lifted. What was before us was unbearable. Folded hands laid on a beautiful white dress. The blond hair was all that could be seen at the top of the dress. Yards and yards of gauze had been wrapped to cover the neck and face from the top of the dress to the hair line. We gasped. I was speechless for words of comfort. The terror of the sight was a living nightmare.

Day Eighteen

The morning of the memorial service came. I was a tortured pastor. The sight of that body in the coffin would not leave my mind. I would be standing behind the body of Debbie who only a few days before had said: "I would make Jesus a priority!" Now at the age of 16 she was to be buried without a face.

If it had not happened to me I might argue the case. But it did happen to me. I started hurting. My constitution is strong.

My tolerance for pain is high. I have had abdominal surgery and never taken pain medicine. But this pain wrecked my body. Try as I might there was no mastery of the pain. I went from being six feet tall to lying in the floor in a fetal position. I went from preparing for a funeral to lying in a hospital with multiple shots of morphine.

My body yielded up a kidney stone. I am convinced that my mind told my body it needed deliverance. My body, while it may have been working on the problem for some time, chose the moment to get my mind out of the nightmare. I could not do the funeral service for Debbie. I was a patient in the hospital heavily sedated, unable to even move of my own accord.

I had only enough time and presence of mind to call an elderly retired minister friend. He came to the rescue and conducted the service.

I will argue that there are times when instead of "mind over matter," it may be "matter over mind." A pastor is called. His passion may be great. However, at the end of the day his body can only bear so much of what the mind loads. The body can just say, "That's enough. I need a break!"

It is best for a pastor to heed warnings before his body says more loudly, "I quit!"

Day 19
The Baptism

Often when a pastor accepts a new charge there is a season of sowing. Then God in His providence provides a season of reaping. The timing is the Lord's. One of the strangest things Laila and I have witnessed is that the season of reaping may be God's sending in what we have called "unearned" people. We reap where we have not sown.

Why I do not know, but Murphy's Law of "If it can go wrong, it will," at times seems to apply. When the sky is gray, the whole world is gray. Yet, when there is sunshine the whole world seems right.

We were having a good season. In this good season a baptismal service was planned. There was excitement in the congregation. A man in his 70's was among those to be baptized. His youth had been spent in a liturgical church. He had been christened as an infant, i.e., water sprinkled on his forehead when he was only a few days old. He did not remember being christened. He wanted to be immersed in water baptism.

It was a joyful experience as person after person came to stand in the baptismal pool and testify of their love for Jesus.

On one side was a lady deacon who directed. On the other side an elder brother sent the men in. Children came first, and then we alternated between men and women.

The final man was Brother Cloman, the elderly brother. There was an air of suspense and praise in the atmosphere. I turned to the elder to indicate it was time for our dear brother to enter the water.

Brother Cloman was one step from the top. One more step and he would have been in full view to a group of widows on the front row on the other side of the church. He was wearing his boxer shorts and a sleeveless t-shirt, neither of which would have fared well when soaking wet.

I was mortified. Looking at Laila at the organ I indicated the need for her to play another verse and play it louder. Holding my hand in the direction of the microphone, being careful not to touch it, I turned to the elder and said, "Do something!"

The elder discreetly motioned with his hands and lip-worded: "What?"

I responded, "Whatever, just do something!"

"He only has his dress clothes," the elder said.

"Put them on him, we will get him home," I replied.

Laila played. We sang. Brother Cloman was relatively ambivalent to the moment of panic. He put on his fine suit and was baptized.

As I was growing up in church it seemed everyone just knew what to do. The sinner that got saved had been to church and knew the routine. Water baptism was public. No one gave instructions. No one had to give instructions. We did not have robes. We baptized in creeks and rivers. Folks just wrapped up and went home.

Day Nineteen

But we were pastoring in a different year and in the city. We discovered that many folks who come to Jesus have never seen a baptism and never read a Bible. So we decided to buy robes.

Laila and I still laugh about that baptismal service. If Brother Cloman had stepped up on the platform, heart attacks might have taken three widows from us. Then we consider the other side of the story. Brother Cloman was not married. We might have had a wedding!

Day 20
Six Dollars and Thirty-Seven Cents

We moved into the parsonage in the Spring of 1973, Laila and I and our two children. Rationally, it made no sense. We were both college graduates--both with debts for our education. Our only income would be from the church, amounting to 75% of the weekly tithe income.

With only six or eight church members working at about $2.00 per hour, how much tithe could we expect? Of course, there were two or three widows who also tithed on Social Security checks of about $300 per month, thus $30 tithe.

We did not sit down and work out a budget. We did not tell the Bishop how much we needed to pay school bills and meet the needs for our family. We simply agreed to pastor the church.

In addition, I was trying to complete graduate work at The College of William and Mary. Balancing all this required me to substitute teach in high school, occasionally buy and sell a car—hopefully making a profit--and a few other mundane odd jobs. A few times I resorted to the paintbrush, having been a commercial contractor during undergraduate days.

Winter came. It was a hard winter. Below zero temperatures. Lots of snow. Times were difficult for us personally, though we did not complain. Nor did we tell the precious people in the congregation. They were doing the best they could do.

Sundays were the best day of the week. Worship services were terrific. It did seem that heaven came down and kissed away all our cares as we sang, prayed, fellowshipped, and preached.

Just before leaving church on Sunday night the clerk would give us our check amounting to 75% of whatever had come in for tithes that week. We had learned over time that we could best hide our reaction if we did not look at the check until after we were home.

On a particular February Sunday evening the clerk, good man that he was, handed me the envelope and there was a trembling in his voice.

"Pastor Bare," he said, "I wish it were more, but that is all there is." He was having a difficult time. I assured him the Lord would provide.

Later, we knelt at our piano bench with Danny and Dana beside us. As was our custom, we put our hands on the unopened envelope and prayed. We asked the Lord to make the amount of the check sufficient to meet our needs for the week. We thanked Him that He would make it so, as He had promised to take care of us.

The moment of reality was now upon us. We opened the envelope to behold a check in the amount of $6.37. If it was cold and dark outside, it suddenly seemed colder and darker.

We cheerfully fed the children and put them to bed. Then we may have allowed ourselves a tear or two, I really don't remember. What I do know was that every week we made it through to the next week. We did make it. The Lord did provide.

Once a woman who was not even a Christian parked her car in front of our home and carried in bag after bag of groceries. "I do not understand it," she said, "I was in the grocery store and something just told me to bring groceries here."

It was almost five years before the clerk came and said: "Pastor Bare, there is enough to pay you a salary for the first time. In fact, here is a check bringing you to salary level for the past three weeks!"

I am grateful for that check of $6.37. Years later I asked the clerk if he could retrieve the cancelled check. Had he been able to, I would have framed it for my office wall. That check is a testimony to God's grace and faithfulness. We were faithful. God was gracious. He met our needs.

Of this I am sure, when ministers have to work long and hard and worry about food for their family, it is not pleasant. Consequently, Laila and I have seek to serve and encourage as many pastors and their families as we can. We want to be Christ's hands and feet extended.

We do not want to forget the days when we had less. We do not want to forget the days when we faithfully preached the gospel without promise of support or sustenance. God's favor must ever drive our hearts to take up our cross and follow Jesus.

His grace is sufficient. The heartfelt kindnesses and efforts of loving people are also priceless encouragements.

Day 21
Surprise Miracles

I am a pastor, the son of a pastor, and married to the daughter of a pastor. I preached my first sermon at age 17. More than 45 years have passed since then. Miracles have come randomly, not every day, not every week, and not every month. There have been seasons that seemed long without divine intervention that provided any story other than faithfulness.

God moves in His timing. Often he has surprised me. Meantime, events that seemed predictable have not happened as I expected.

Take the case of Sister Kegley. Some time after she had borrowed and loaned money to the church she was with a group of ladies in the church fellowship hall on a weekday. As I drove back into the church parking lot a person ran out of the church doors saying: "Pastor, come quickly. Something awful is happening to Sister Kegley!"

I ran into the church and bounded down the steps two or three at a time. A voice seemed to speak in my ear: "It is not her time to die." When I rounded the corner into the room it was too late, according to my eyes. Sister Kegley was dead. Her head was back. Her eyes were rolled to the whites. Her tongue was protruded. She slid into the floor lifeless. I felt for a pulse, even putting my ear to her chest below her chin—neither hearing nor feeling pulse. I had seen people die. She was dead.

There was that voice again, "It is not her time to die."

I was panicky. What was God doing to me? I am no Moses or Elijah. Why would God play games with me? It is a fearful thing to be caught in the straights between God and one's own fear of God. Suppose God was up to something and I did not cooperate?

I needed a plan to protect my integrity. Looking up at the people around I gave rapid-fire instructions. "Go call the ambulance. Go open doors to the church. Go move cars to allow the ambulance to pull directly to the doors of the building. Check with the golf course across the road and see if there is a doctor there."

With persons gone to care for the assigned tasks, there were still some people left, frightened and weeping people.

I motioned for those not assigned to duty to go to a far corner and pray. Looking around to make sure no one was listening, I knelt down beside the dead body and whispered into a lifeless ear as I took the advice of Ezekiel: "Sister Kegley, God said it is not your time to die. If you can hear my voice think upon the Name of Jesus. Say it in your mind. Repeat the Name of Jesus," and thus I continued, always with a furtive eye to make sure that no one was coming near.

I was in fear of God, and I also had little hope of a dead woman's coming to life. I feared being called a fool.

There was a little motion. Her body seemed to move. She began to breathe ever so slowly.

The ambulance came. Medics rushed to find Sis. Kegley sitting up on the floor speaking in other tongues as the Spirit gave

Day Twenty-One

utterance (Acts 2:8). They took her to the hospital where she stayed in intensive care for several days.

Dr. Stone shared with me when I picked her up to take her home: "Reverend, medical knowledge tells us that something awful happened to this woman. However, try as we might we cannot determine what it was. It seems she was dead. But the fingerprints are all gone. Just take her home and be thankful."

When I hear ministers tell stories that always make them sound like a hero, I tend to remember Sister Kegley's coming to life. I was no hero. I was a frightened and obedient servant who did not expect a miracle. I was human. Still am. I'm glad God uses human vessels.

Day 22
The Red Necktie

Out of graduate school, Laila and I were sure of my placement in immigration work. Even so, every door closed. The door opened for us to pastor a congregation of about 65 people on Sunday mornings. We entered.

Progress was steady and attendance almost doubled. I knew that unless the congregation cared about the larger mission of the world there was not much hope for us to grow larger. One Sunday my heart was set on communicating that Jesus went a'fishing.

I called a parishioner that I knew had fishing rods. He brought a fishing rod about eight feet long. Leaning the fishing rod against the pulpit I read scripture about Jesus going out and choosing disciples, especially Levi. "Follow me," Jesus said as he walked by, and "Lo, (Levi) rose, left all, and followed him" [Luke 5:28].

Central to the message was that Jesus was a fisherman who fished for men, women, and children. He went looking for people to join the Kingdom.

The message seemed to be going well. In an energetic moment I stepped out of the pulpit with the fishing rod in my left hand. Down the aisle I came with the congregation intensely listening and watching. It was one of those joyous times when a pastor feels the Holy Spirit doing a good work.

In a moment of spontaneity I searched in my heart for a way to bring the most powerful point of the sermon home. A fisherman baits and casts the line. Whatever hooks the line is reeled in. The more the struggle on the end of the line, the greater the joy of the fisherman to net the fish. Oh, the sermon was going well.

That's when I looked on my right and there was Grandpa Lewis. He rarely spoke. He was meek. He loved his pastor. And, he was wearing a red necktie. With the fishing rod in my left hand, I reached with my right hand and took hold of Grandpa's red necktie. "Jesus, will come fishing for you because He loves you, but Jesus will never force you to follow him!" I said as I gave a little pull on Grandpa's necktie.

What I had not figured was that Grandpa's necktie was a clip-on. There I stood in the center of the aisle with a fishing rod in my left hand a red necktie dangling in my right hand. The congregation erupted in laughter. My associate on stage was laughing so hard he almost fell out of his chair.

Well, there was nothing to do but accept the moment. I gave Grandpa his necktie. By God's grace the Holy Spirit gave me an insight how to pull the message together. The service ended well, though more than a few folks left with a little smile on their faces.

More than 20 years have passed. The Red Necktie Story is sometimes recalled by parishioners. I laugh along with them. It was a funny moment.

It was also a helpful moment. Preaching a sermon has dynamics that cannot always be anticipated. One has the choice of being liturgical, reading a sermon, employing professional skills

Day Twenty-Two

of inflection of voice and motion of hands and body language. Or one has the choice, frightfully so, of being prepared and yet allowing the Holy Spirit to influence presentation.

If a formal presentation is chosen, then the congregation is not likely to be highly excited about Sunday morning sermons. If a pastor opts for some spontaneity guided by the Holy Spirit, the probability of surprise moments increases.

One thing sure, whichever method of operation a pastor chooses for delivery of sermons there will be moments when events will take their own course. A pastor will do well to have a good sense of humor and keep in mind that people have good memories. Sometimes the most memorable is the unusual, like a preacher with a fishing rod in one hand and Grandpa's red necktie in the other.

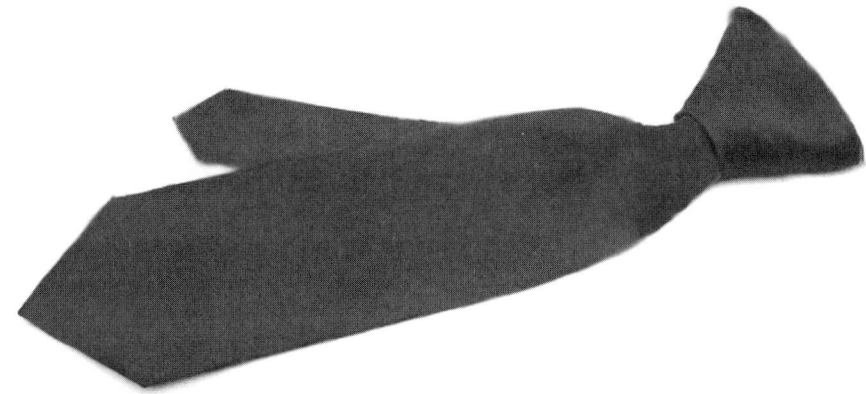

Day 23
Wendall

Wendall was a Vietnam veteran who had grown up in church and been very devoted to Jesus during his childhood and youth. War and war injuries brought Wendall home with full disability payment, a bright mind, dependence on drugs, and an obsession with religion.

He could still walk, drive, read, watch TV, and piddle at a little work, though the idea of work repulsed him. His disability income from war injuries was sufficient for a good life. He and his wife could sleep as late as they wanted to, eat out, and drive a better car than most people. They had very little debt if any. Money, though not in great supply, was enough to offer opportunities not common to neighbors.

Wendall did not attend our church. He lived several miles away in a mountain village. However, unfortunately for me—much of the time, our phones were on a local system.

He was obsessed with prophecy. Like as not my phone would ring after midnight [when TV station used to sign off], and he would say: "Pastor, I was just thinking about the Great Tribulation period. What do you think the seven thunders is really about?"

Our relationship was candid. I cared that he was a veteran. He had likable qualities. In his family were good church folks who were part of our network. But to his midnight musings I might respond: "Wendall, get off this phone and go to bed. I am not interested in seven thunders at two AM."

He responded: "But I can't sleep."

I replied: "Fine, I will call you when I get up. Then you can get up. Then you stay up all day. Work in your garden. Leave the TV off. I will call you when I go to bed. Then you can go to bed, and you will sleep like I want to be asleep."

Don't be judgmental. You had to know Wendall. He was not offended. He would call again. His musings ranged from seven thunders questions to observations that I should have a TV ministry and buy a helicopter to fly to my appointments.

One day a call came. "Wendall is missing," was the message. "His medicine is messed up. He is drinking hard liquor, and he has a gun. Do you know where he is? If you hear from him, please call immediately."

It was not long before Wendall called me. He did not know that I was aware of the police APB. We began to talk. He was a mental mess. "Will you talk to me and not hang up?" he asked.

I hemmed and hawwed as folks would say in the hollow. Delaying. He continued: "But you cannot say that Name."

"What Name?" I asked, as if I did not know.

"You know the Name I am talking about," he said. "If you say that Name I will have to hang up."

"Well," I ambled along. "Seems to me that if I have to keep promises you too must be part of the contract. If I do not say that Name, you must promise not to hang up on me."

Day Twenty-Three

We negotiated and settled on terms. All the while I was writing notes to Laila. Laila was running across the street to a neighbor's home and talking with the Sheriff's department. The Sheriff's office was working with the phone company and traced the call to a motel in the area.

Suddenly, Wendall's voice became frantic. "Somebody is outside my room," he said. "I must hang up."

"You can't hang up," I said very commandingly. "We have a contract. I kept my bargain. You have to keep yours. Now, lay the phone down, peek through the curtains, come back to the phone and tell me what you see."

There were lots of police cars and officers. I instructed him to lay the phone down and stay in his bed until I arrived. Phoning the Sheriff's department I informed them I was on my way to the motel.

It was not easy to convince the police officers that a preacher should go alone to talk with Wendall. They finally agreed. Officers withdrew. I asked Wendall to stand behind the door and unlatch it. He did. I eased into the room and closed the door.

He fell back onto his bed, clad only in his shorts. Drugs were on the nightstand. An almost empty whisky bottle was beside a loaded pistol easily within his reach. I did not feel safe.

I also did not know what to do. All I knew was that I would rather be hurt than have Wendall and others shot.

Moving very slowly, I picked up a large bath towel and turned on the coldwater faucet. My thought was that I would wet the towel thoroughly and then wrap it around his feet. Maybe the coldness would bring some soberness to his mind.

When I began to kneel at his feet with the towel he suddenly exclaimed: "You cannot do that!"

There was a moment of panic. I calmly said: "Why not?"

"I am not worthy," he said.

It was a wondrous moment. My coldwater theory to produce soberness had planted a seed in his mind of past memories. He thought I was preparing to wash his feet as Jesus washed the feet of the disciples.

The wonder of how the Holy Spirit helps preachers never ceases to amaze me. I later walked out with a clothed Wendall, mind much settled, and the officers agreed to allow me to drive him home. God had done His work.

Pastors serve a lot of people that never sit in their pews nor put a dime in the offering plate of their parish.

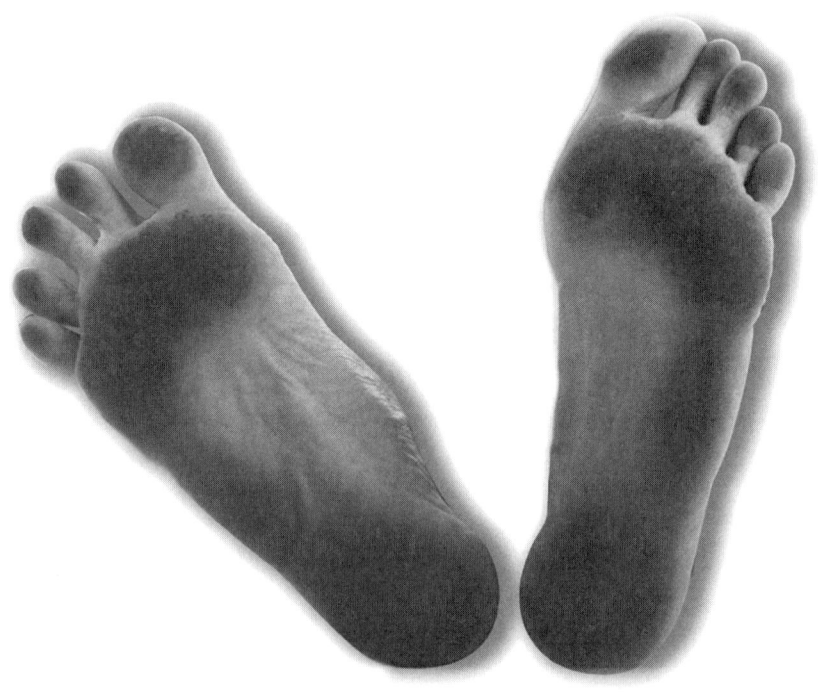

Day 24
Talking To the Bishop

We were in a building program. Total cost was about $70,000, but the value was $200,000. Men in the church did carpentry in the evenings and Saturday. We hauled materials, dug ditches, and assisted sub-contractors to save every nickel possible.

Personal friends of mine did work in the coalfields. When I told them we needed some grading done they unloaded a 1957 Caterpillar front-end loader. "Climb up here, Preacher. I will teach you about this machine." For an hour or so both of us were on the machine.

"When will an operator arrive?" I asked.

"Operator? You did not ask for an operator. I will teach you how to operate the machine. Climb up here. Learn. Keep it full of fuel and run the engine strong. When you are through with the machine, call me for pickup." He was gone.

When we were through with the front-end loader he bought a new backhoe and delivered it to the church. I learned again.

But one day carrying the world on my shoulders seemed very tiring. A building program can wear on a pastor. I later learned that most pastors leave their position within a year after a large building program.

I got in my old car and drove over to the city where my district Bishop pastored. Ours was one of six churches under his immediate supervision. Walking into a million dollar new sanctuary and plush offices (that was 1970's), I asked to see the Bishop. He had a suite—private restroom, shower, receptionist, and even an apartment off from his office for rest.

"How can I help you, Pastor?" he asked. Then he leaned back in his executive chair, laid his head back as if in deep thought, and clasped his hands on top of his tummy which still protruded upward even with his backward tilt. He seemed a page to be written on.

I talked. I was not depressed. I was not ready to quit. I was not mad. I had no sad stories to tell. I was tired. I simply needed a listening ear, an encouraging word, and a Bishop to make me feel included in the big circle of brotherhood. It can be lonely on the frontier. It can be especially lonely during a building program. It can be frightfully lonely when a building program is financially challenged.

I poured out my heart. No weeping. No flailing of arms. Just an honest rendering of thoughts, opinions, and anxieties. He listened. No comments. No approbation. No correction. He just listened. I came to a stopping point. I wanted to hear him speak.

"Well, Pastor," he said without moving, though he did fully open his eyes, "When you get where I am you will see that all that you are going through is good for you. You will see things differently." His hands still rested on that big tummy.

Day Twenty-Four

I am not proud of what happened next. It was not long before I went out the door. I was frustrated and had a few other emotions that are best left unsaid. To this day I can show you where I was on Interstate 81 when I made a pledge to myself: "I will never again open my heart to talk to another person like I did today!"

Arriving home and greeting Laila she asked, "How did it go?"

"Sweetheart, put on the beans and 'tators. The Bishop rested his hands on his big tummy and said I would not understand until I get where he is. I must gain a lot of weight!"

We laughed. We made it through the building program. In time I retracted my rash promise not to confide in advisors.

The Bishop did me a great favor that day. He caused me to see how easy it is to become pompous and arrogant in ministry. Laila and I have made a covenant that we want to ever give ourselves away to help other pastors and ministers. It is our desire to encourage, and our hope that our caring will prevent many from experiencing much of the pain we have endured.

We are but servants—unprofitable servants [Luke 17:10]. We can never repay what the Lord has done for us.

Day 25
The Newcomer

Because I was helping a person he had abused, a man had threatened to kill me. He was capable. His criminal record was such that the Sheriff for our community gave special protection orders for me. A squad car was to be within five minutes every night. I was to call if anything was suspicious.

Security alerts and training were done with key parishioners who had special training. Even during Sunday worship there were professional eyes making sure that no stranger came into our congregation to do harm. At the time our elder son Danny was 13 years old. He remembers my instructions: "If you ever see an orange pickup, get your sister and brother, run to a safe place, and call the police."

Being threatened as a pastor is not unusual. However, to have someone issue a direct "I will rip that preacher's jugular veins out with my bare hands," was a little much. Our family was ever careful. Laila did not want to be a widow at such a young age.

Our family home was an apartment, part of the church complex. The master bedroom was beside a sidewalk that led to the main entrance door of the church. We could look out our window across the parking lot to the main highway.

"There is someone outside," Laila whispered.

"Sweetheart, it is one o'clock in the morning. There is no one outside," I responded.

"There is someone out there. See for yourself. I can hear them," she continued.

Without turning on a light I sat on the side of the bed and opened the curtains just enough to see that a man was walking across the parking lot directly toward our bedroom window. It did not matter that the entrance door to the church was just past our window. The church was dark, locked and with no one inside. We were alive and in the path of an unknown visitor.

Easing the curtain back together I felt for the telephone. By touch I found zero. A voice answered. I said: "Operator, emergency. Please connect me to the police department."

When the next voice answered I said: "This is Pastor Bare. We have an unidentified man coming toward our bedroom window."

We looked at the digital clock, the only light in the darkness. One minute passed. A squad car slid sideways in the main road with lights flashing. One minute later another squad car entered the church parking lot and virtually slid sideways with red light flashing. Two minutes later another squad car with red lights flashing came further into the church lot.

An officer with gun drawn called out to the unidentified man: "Put your hands in the air!" Hands went up. Officers carefully approached.

"Identify yourself and why you are here," an officer gave a sharp order.

With hands still in the air the man gave his name in a rather frightened voice and said, "I was supposed to pick up my brother from an AA meeting, but I am late and apparently lost."

Day Twenty-Five

Dressing hurriedly, I went outside. After hearing the explanation, I apologized to the young man. A sincere effort was made to invite him back to our worship services. I did everything imaginable to assure him of our caring for and about him. In spite of all my efforts he never came back.

Often I reflect upon that episode of the first-time visitor. Many folks stop by just once. We must put our best foot forward when a first-time visitor comes. Yet, with every effort given, some will not return. Some come to leave and nothing we can do will cause them to stay. It is no fault of the pastor or the people that some folks come by with an agenda. Their agenda is not the agenda of the pastor and the congregation.

They are visiting for their own motive. They only came for what they wanted, not what they needed. They won't come back.

Newcomers don't always stay. Don't expect it.

Day 26
That Woman

I am grateful for Laila. The Lord gave me a good companion, friend, and wife. She is wise and a good wife for a pastor.

We are normal. Our children were not ordered from Sears Department Store. We procreated.

Once Laila observed to me that she thought another woman was attractive. "What do you think?" she asked me. I, of course, pretended that I had not even seen the woman, much less observed whether she was attractive or ugly. Laila candidly brought balance to the awkward moment.

"If I ask you whether you think another woman is attractive, I want an honest answer," she said.

Inching now toward forty-two years of marriage we have had to work through many issues. Most of them will never be written about, though the happiness grows.

One issue that needs attention is That Woman. I like to think of myself as a prudent man. In the old days ministers never hugged a woman, nor allowed anything more than a polite handshake. These new times have been something of a challenge.

Ours is a trans-cultural congregation. Many of the ethnic or cultural groups have the social interaction of greeting each other with a hug, a cheek-to-cheek, even a kiss. Well do I remember the time when a woman warmly greeted her pastor with a handshake and cheek-to-cheek with a little smacking sound—a kiss? Didn't seem like the lips touched the skin. So much I don't know. What I do know is that a dear lady of another culture was nearby and almost fainted. Needless to say our congregation has had to grow a lot in understanding different cultures.

How does Laila play into all this challenge and change? Well, Laila and I have an understanding. A few times in our 30 plus years of being a pastor's family, a woman has come along that makes me awfully nervous. Don't ask me the particulars. I have not figured out all the details.

All I know is that there is a feeling That Woman is out to get closer to me than I feel comfortable. If she can get close to me she has a way of putting her hand on my arm, or wanting to hug me face forward.

If you think that I am of the opinion I am irresistible, forget it. Not so. I am just human. Married. Only have room in my heart and life for one woman.

The truth of the matter is that Laila laughs at me when That Woman starts in my direction. Laila says she can see the reaction in my eyes as my body tenses, and before I give her the signal she knows I am calling for help.

That's right. When That Woman comes into our congregation I forthrightly tell Laila. I ask Laila to put up a wall between me and That Woman. It is understood that Laila will stay in the area if That Woman is around. If That Woman starts angling in my direction, Laila is to be by my side before That Woman arrives.

Day Twenty-Six

That Woman has sure brought a lot of misery to a lot of preachers' lives. I have no intention of being another statistic. I am married. I like being married. Laila fills my heart.

If you have never experienced meeting That Woman, you are blessed. However, do not be smug. That Woman cares not about how old or good looking a minister is. She only cares to get through to the human part, the flesh. Wait until the finish line before you boast of being so strong.

Meanwhile, it will serve you well to make sure that you and your spouse, if you have one, are well connected. Work at a relationship that your spouse can be an honest partner to come to the rescue in time of need. Work at honesty to insure that trust is not a question between you and your spouse.

That Woman is out there somewhere. Put up fences to keep her at a safe distance.

Day 27
World's Worst Sermon

More preachers than you think have tried to take the credit for preaching the "World's Worst Sermon." There is no need to question or argue. No need to hold a contest. I hold the title!

It was Sunday night. Those good folks deserved better. What went wrong? I can't remember. All I remember is that as the sermon came to a close I came to the conclusion that the presentation did not deserve grading. It does not matter that others did not judge the sermon so poorly. I was the preacher. I knew it was The World's Worst Sermon!

During the benediction I did the unorthodox and slipped out the side door of the sanctuary. "Amen" found me absent. I was already out the door and into our apartment within the church building. In the darkness I made my way to the bedroom and quietly sat down in a rocking chair.

Voices of people talking on the sidewalk just outside my window could be heard. I imagined what was being said. There was no wish in my mind for folks to pine at the funeral of a supposedly dead Tom Sawyer. My hope was they would go home.

Laila came into the house and called for me. I did not answer. When she made her way to the bedroom and turned on the lights I calmly said: "Please leave the lights off." She did.

"What is happening? Are you alright?" she asked.

"I am fine," I responded, "but I just preached the world's worst sermon and do not want to see anyone tonight. I will get over it, but I do not want to talk with people. Just let them go home."

What a wonderful wife. She eased back out the door and said a quiet goodbye to the last of the folks. Then she came in to assure me that the sermon was not as bad as I thought. Ah, my Number One supporter.

It was our second pastorate. We had been there about a year. In the first eight months we had completed an 8,000 square foot building program with considerable volunteer labor. Maybe I was just tired. Maybe the long hours and financial strain had gotten to me.

Monday night came. A meeting was called by about a dozen parishioners. They did not ask me. They did not invite me. They initiated the meeting and the agenda: "How do we get the load off of our pastor?"

Just before the dismissal that Sunday night while still in front of the whole congregation, I had requested the soundman destroy the only tape of the sermon. No one can affirm or deny my claim to the title of "The World's Worst Sermon" with any factual evidence.

However, time has caused me to reflect upon my feelings about a sermon and my very human reaction to feelings of failure. "The World's Worst Sermon" resulted in many parishioners getting involved in ministry like no other sermon I had preached.

Day Twenty-Seven

That meeting on a Monday night set our parish on a course of action that became more about folks in the pews and less about the person in the pulpit. Respect for the pastor increased. Out of that terrible and awful sermon folks decided that a pastor should not have to mow the lawn, do all the visitation, and see every patient in the hospital, in addition to preaching, teaching, and other duties.

Good laity opened their eyes to see that much of what is done in a church, in fact, most of what is done in ministry, can be done by anyone willing to be used of the Holy Spirit. Those good folks decided that laity helping is the biblical path. When the pew and the pulpit get together in partnership awesome things happen.

One thing sure: If I knew how to preach another World's Worst Sermon that would have the impact of that sermon so long ago, I would. But this time I would stay for the benediction.

Day 28
We Never Cancel

As I pick up the teddy bear and press his hand, I can't help but smile as I hear him speak in the youth pastor's familiar voice, "We never close!" Some time ago the teens brought him to me from one of their retreats. He has a special place on my office shelf.

Our parish is located in a four-season climate. Though none of our seasons are really severe, winter weather is the most likely to prevent safe travel.

One of my great frustrations is the tendency of churches to close in inclement weather. If a weatherman on Friday forecasts snow on Sunday, many churches announce closing before the snow begins. I have known pastors and leaders to call off church for rain, for sports events, for family reunions, and simply to give people a day off.

At the beginning of this long-term pastorate, I decided that our doors to worship would never be closed on a Sunday. "We Never Cancel" is part of our motto. Weather never shuts our doors.

If necessary my wife and I spend the night or weekend at the church. Sunday morning the steps are cleared. At least a small path is cleared down the sidewalk, and the sanctuary is heated and lighted.

One Sunday almost a foot of snow had fallen—enough snow to challenge road equipment. Laila looked out the window about daylight and said: "Honey, I think this time you will have to call it."

That ole Tarheel spirit rose up within me: "Not canceling. We open." A parishioner came to the church in a four-wheel truck. He was also a heavy equipment operator. The ground was so frozen he used a bulldozer to push snow off the church parking lot. That was quite a sight to see!

Folks came. The word got out that we were not canceling worship service. More folks came. Folks from other denominations came. We had a wonderful congregation. Wonderful worship. Wonderful offering. Wonderful fellowship.

When we walked out of church it was over 50 degrees. The sun was shining. The sudden and unexpected warm-up had allowed roads to be cleared.

Seven churches were along our road within one mile. We were the only congregation that had a worship service.

Oh, sure, I know that does not make us heroes. It did not make us more saintly than saints who could not go to church. But it did get a message out. We were serious about not canceling worship services.

One Sunday my son and I made it to church. We waited. The main road was so bad that the snow had not been plowed. Snow was almost to the knees of a grown man.

Time for worship came. As Danny and I were preparing to share scripture and have prayer, the doors opened. In came a medical doctor and his teenage son. "Pastor," the doctor said,

Day Twenty-Eight

"I am so glad you are here. I worked a 30-hour medical shift. Someone took me home. My car is stuck in the snow. But I told my wife that I had to go to church. I needed to be in church. My son wanted to come with me. We have walked three miles in the snow just to be in church, and we knew you would be here!"

We had a wonderful time of worship with a congregation of four.

Many times I have sat in the office on a cold snowy/icy morning and waited. The phone would ring: "Good morning, Pastor Bare. How may I help you?"

The response would be: "Oh, Pastor, I cannot make it today, but I just wanted to hear your voice. I knew that someone would be there at the church. That means so much to me."

Others will in good conscience choose their course. However, for me the course is set: We Never Cancel!

Day 29
Big Red

He was not as big as he thought he was. His ego was huge. In reality he was only about five feet nine inches tall. His beer belly, as folks call it in the country where I grew up, protruded ugly.

But with cowboy boots, a huge western buckle holding his jeans, a working shirt and baseball cap, he swaggered as if he were the mayor of the town.

I knew him for the rascal that he was. He beat his wife. He threatened to kill his children. Often the children would run and hide when they heard their belligerent and abusive drunken father coming down the country road.

His first marriage had gone south. Reportedly, he had loved that woman, but she tired of his ways and found another lover. In the fallout she took him to the cleaners for hundreds of thousands of dollars. He was bitter. Unforgiving. He would talk about how much he loved his first wife and the money she took with her all in the same breath. It was difficult to separate the love and hate.

His second wife got the hate. He worked her like a slave. He held on to the money and made her ask for a few dollars even for personal items. He checked grocery money and receipts. It was not being thrifty. It was greed. No judgment on my part. He ran illegal tags, sold drugs, and a few other things to make money and avoid taxes.

I have never told anyone to get a divorce. Not my calling. I have more than once advised a woman to get out of her home with her children and to safety for a season. I told Big Red's wife to leave the home and take the children to a safe place. He was exhibiting dangerous signs of violence.

"Get to safety. Leave a path that I can get in touch with you, but do not give me the details," were my final instructions.

She obeyed. Not long after my phone rang. It was Big Red. Big Red would not come to church. He hated church. He hated anything and anybody that seemed to get between him and his despotic control of his wife and children.

"Preacher," he said without respect, "Do you know where my wife and children are?"

"Big Red, I cannot talk with you unless you come to my office," I said flatly and firmly.

Oh, that was a hatchet in the sand. He was mad. He ventilated. It was not nice what he said. I stood my ground.

He came to the church. I insisted he come into the office. The rules for the office with the "Pastor" sign on the door are that no one be allowed to stand up and talk business, and that no one is to speak with voices raised in anger. I insisted that he sit down and lower his voice.

Have you ever seen a blow fish? When it gets upset it swells up like it is pumped full of air. That was Big Red. He was coiled, tense, red in the face, and mad as hornets after a rock has been thrown into the nest.

Day Twenty-Nine

He sat on the edge of the chair, feet spread apart, turned his hands backwards and pressed them against his knees as if he would spring on me at any moment.

"Let's get something straight. I don't like this church. I don't like you. I don't want to be here. And I don't trust nobody." He spit it out with vengeance drawing the battle lines.

Not surprised I leaned back into my chair, pausing a moment for reflection and prayer. Then I leaned strongly in his direction. Looking him directly in the eye I said: "Fair enough. Any man who does not trust himself ought not trust anybody!"

Laughing, he said: "I think I could get to like you."

It took years and more losses for Big Red to recognize his weaknesses and need of church and God. His story has not been a happy book.

What I do know is that pastors do not win every battle. There are heart-breaking losses. More than once I have lost friends who departed life without any testimony of salvation. The sight of one cemetery in our community always brings a fresh sorrow for a friend who committed suicide. He was a good man in many ways, but he allowed a bad woman to use him until he was obsessed.

One night we sat on his porch until midnight as I ministered to him and pleaded with him to turn his heart to Jesus. I did not succeed in convincing him.

Pastors do well to face their work with a sense of reality. People are people. People make choices. Some choose righteousness. Others choose evil. A pastor who counts victories instead of defeats is wise and will have joy.

Day 30
Running Away

Dana, our only daughter, was about age 4 when she felt some injustice in her life. Looking at me she calmly said: "I am going to run away from home." No anger. No malice. She was just going to leave us. Go away.

"Well, Darling, [Oh, how I love that little girl], you cannot just run away. There is a proper way to run away. If you insist that this is something you must do, Daddy will help you."

"First," I said, "You need a red bandanna."

Together we went in search of the bandanna. When we had found one I spread it on her bed, pressed it out with my hands and explained: "Now you must gather a few things that are precious to you. Place them on the bandanna, and then come and get Daddy."

I left her alone for the awful task of sorting through her valuables. When she came for me I found a few small bottles of perfume and tiny soaps.

"Is this all?" I asked. She nodded her head.

"Next thing we must do is go and find a stick. Come with me. This is a very important part of running away."

Outside we went in search of a stick about two feet long. It had to be smooth, so it would not press into her shoulder, yet it would be strong enough to hold the bandanna with her valuables and also fit into her little hand.

Back into the house we went. "Next thing," I explained to her, "we must tie the bandanna to the stick."

Taking two corners of the bandanna we tied them into a knot around the end of the stick. The other two corners tied made a nice little package.

Taking her outside I placed the stick on her shoulder with the package behind her. Taking her little hand I placed it around the stick and explained that she would have to hold it firmly and always protect her valuables while traveling.

Kneeling down, I gave her a little hug. Kissed her. Told her how much we loved her. Explained how much we would miss her. "But I understand this is something you need to do," I said. "So, Goodbye, Darling," and I waved her away.

Back in the house I peeped out the window to observe what would happen. Without hesitation she set out as if on a journey. Down the yard she went. I moved from place to place in the house to keep an eye on her. She proceeded to go all the way around the house at least twice.

The door opened. She came in and went to her room. I did not unwrap the bandanna. She did. She put her things up. She decided to stay home.

Oh, there have been Sundays when I have picked up the classifieds of the newspaper and looked at needs of universities for professors. I have even guardedly talked with persons who needed certain professional skills, and otherwise exhibited the Elijah syndrome of "Let me die," or otherwise translated, "Get me out of here!"

Day Thirty   117

I have mentally put a few things in a bandanna, tied them to a stick and walked around the church imagining another time and place where things could be better, easier, more fulfilling, and with less stress. Especially on those Sundays when things did not go so well I have wanted to run away.

"And thinking back it seems to me that the Holy Spirit was as gentle to me as a daddy with his little girl who wanted to run away. Once when contemplating possible alternatives to being a pastor, I felt the Holy Spirit gently prompt me: "My child, in large print I made plain your appointment as a pastor. Why are you reading small print about running away? When it is time for you to go I will print marching orders in large print."

I got rid of my stick and bandanna many Sundays ago.

An Invitation

Do YOU have a story that would make others smile? Or pause and reflect? Or be glad that God's providential hand was upon you when you went through a valley?

Would you like to be part of the next book? As you have read some of my stories, I hope you have looked into your own rearview mirror and seen stories of God's providence and humor in your life.

This book is intended as the first in a series. You may become a part of the adventure by sharing your own story. E-mail us harold@MyBlueGooseStory.com or write us at 1025 East Rio Road, Charlottesville, VA 22901.

You do not have to write the story—just tell us. If your story is accepted, we'll put it in printed form. If you prefer to write it, that's fine too! Just so long as we are permitted to adapt it for the book.

Everyone—both those in the pulpit and those in the pew—has stories. Share yours!

Dr. Harold L. Bare, Sr.

www.MyBlueGooseStory.com
harold@MyBlueGooseStory.com
laila@MyBlueGooseStory.com